Pebble™

My World

In My
Country

by Heather Adamson

Consulting Editor: Gail Saunders-Smith, PhD
Consultant: Susan B. Neuman, EdD
Former U.S. Assistant Secretary for Elementary
and Secondary Education
Professor, Educational Studies, University of Michigan

Capstone
press
Mankato, Minnesota

Pebble Books are published by Capstone Press,
151 Good Counsel Drive, P.O. Box 669, Mankato, Minnesota 56002.
www.capstonepress.com

1 2 3 4 5 6 10 09 08 07 06 05

Library of Congress Cataloging-in-Publication Data
Adamson, Heather, 1974–
    In my country / by Heather Adamson.
    p. cm.—(Pebble Books. My world)
    Includes bibliographical references and index.
    ISBN 0-7368-4236-5 (hardcover)
    1. Geography—Juvenile literature. I. Title. II. Series: My world (Mankato,
Minn.)
G133.A33 2006
910—dc22   2004030959

Summary: Simple text and photographs introduce basic community concepts
related to countries including location, features of a country, and information about
other countries.

Note to Parents and Teachers

The My World set supports national social studies standards related
to community. This book describes and illustrates basic community
concepts related to countries. The images support early readers in
understanding the text. The repetition of words and phrases helps
early readers learn new words. This book also introduces early
readers to subject-specific vocabulary words, which are defined in
the Glossary section. Early readers may need assistance to read
some words and to use the Table of Contents, Glossary, Read More,
Internet Sites, and Index sections of the book.

Table of Contents

My Country

My country is
the United States
of America.

A country is
made of the land
and the people
who live there.

United States

Texas

I live in the
state of Texas.
Texas is one
of the 50 states
in the United States.

10

Places in My Country

My country's government meets in Washington, D.C. This city is the capital of the United States.

My country has
national parks.
Many people visit
the parks every year.

14

Other Countries

The world has
many countries.
Some countries are hot.
Other countries are cold.

Every country has
its own flag.
A flag is a symbol
of a country.

Japan
yen

Mexico
peso

United States
dollar

Many countries
use their own money.
The United States
uses the dollar.

The United States
is my country.
What do you know
about your country?

Glossary

capital—the city in a country where the government is based

country—an area of land where people live and have a government

government—the people and laws that run a town, state, country, or other area

state—an area of land with borders you can see only on a map; each state can make some of their own laws.

symbol—an object that reminds people of something else; the U.S. flag is a symbol of the United States.

Read More

Nelson, Robin. *Where Is My Country? Where Am I?* Minneapolis: Lerner, 2002.

Schroeder, Holly. *United States ABCs: A Book about the People and Places of the United States.* Country ABCs. Minneapolis: Picture Window Books, 2004.

Internet Sites

FactHound offers a safe, fun way to find Internet sites related to this book. All of the sites on FactHound have been researched by our staff.

Here's how:

1. Visit *www.facthound.com*

2. Type in this special code **0736842365** for age-appropriate sites. Or enter a search word related to this book for a more general search.

3. Click on the **Fetch It** button.

FactHound will fetch the best sites for you!

Index

Word Count: 119
Grade: 1
Early-Intervention Level: 11

Editorial Credits
Mari C. Schuh, editor; Juliette Peters, designer and illustrator; Jo Miller, photo researcher; Scott Thoms, photo editor

Photo Credits
Art Directors/H. Gariety, 4 (background)
Bruce Coleman Inc./Lee Lyon, 14 (top)
Capstone Press/Karon Dubke, cover, 1 (foreground), 4 (foreground), 20 (foreground)
Capstone Press Archives, 18
Corbis/Steve Kanfman, 12; Steve Raymer, 14 (bottom)
David R. Frazier Photolibrary, 10
Folio Inc., 16
Houserstock/Ben R. Frakes, 6
The Image Finders/Patti McConville, 20 (background)
Unicorn Stock Photos/Aneal Vohra, 1 (background)